i explore

SHARKS

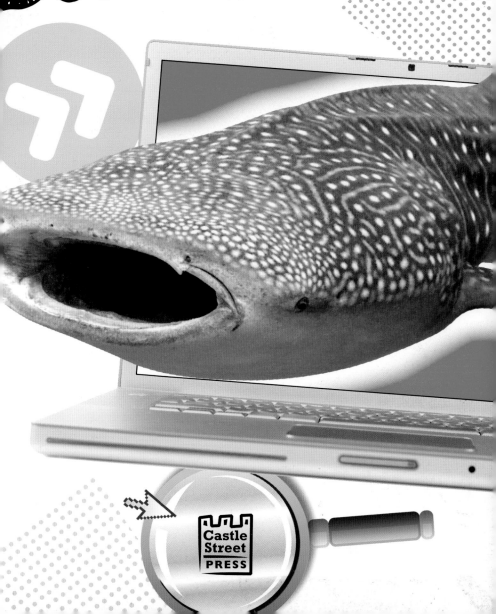

Castle
Street
PRESS

WHAT'S INSIDE?

Discover more about the amazing world of sharks!

Sharks

Hammerhead sha

Unusual shar

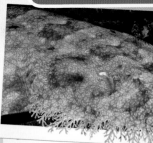

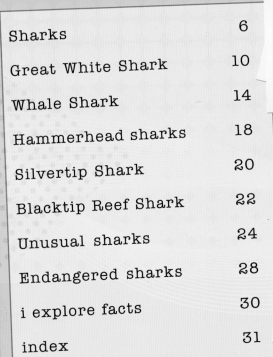

Great White Shark

Whale Shark

Blacktip Reef Shark

Silvertip Shark

Endangered sharks

i explore facts

i explore

SHARKS

There are about 450 types of sharks all over the world, including the gigantic Whale Shark, the spotted Zebra Shark, and the unforgettable Great White Shark.

tail fin

i learn

Sharks use their fins to move in different ways: the tail fin pushes the shark forward, the pectoral fins help the shark to steer through the water, and the dorsal fin helps the shark to balance.

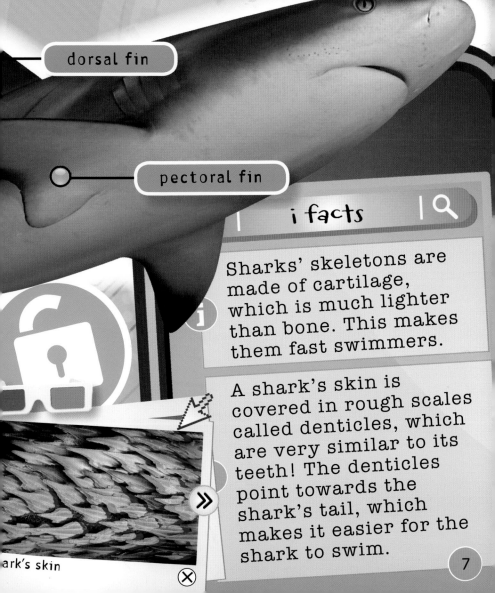

Most sharks have dark-colored skin on the top half of their bodies, while their undersides are pale. A dark color helps them blend in to the water when seen from above, while a pale color helps them blend in to the sky when they are seen from below.

dorsal fin

pectoral fin

i facts

Sharks' skeletons are made of cartilage, which is much lighter than bone. This makes them fast swimmers.

A shark's skin is covered in rough scales called denticles, which are very similar to its teeth! The denticles point towards the shark's tail, which makes it easier for the shark to swim.

ark's skin

The Thresher Shark's tail fin can grow up to 10 ft (3 m) long. Its tail fin can be as long as its whole body!

GREAT WHITE SHARK

The Great White Shark is an excellent hunter. Like all sharks, the Great White uses all of its senses to hunt and catch its prey, including the ability to sense electricity!

i fact

ℹ Sharks don't chew their food – they swallow it whole or in large chunks!

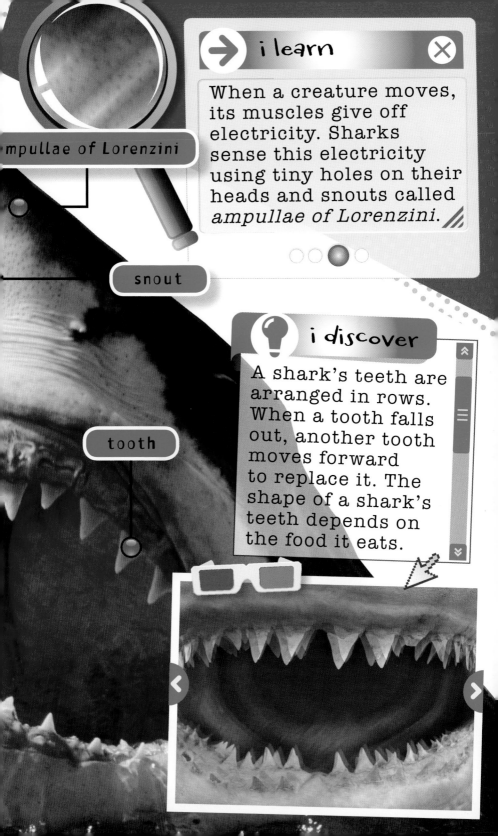

→ i learn ⊗

When a creature moves, its muscles give off electricity. Sharks sense this electricity using tiny holes on their heads and snouts called *ampullae of Lorenzini*.

mpullae of Lorenzini

snout

💡 i discover

A shark's teeth are arranged in rows. When a tooth falls out, another tooth moves forward to replace it. The shape of a shark's teeth depends on the food it eats.

tooth

i fact

Sharks hunt in different ways. The Great White Shark circles prey just below the surface of the sea. When it is ready to strike, it attacks from underneath!

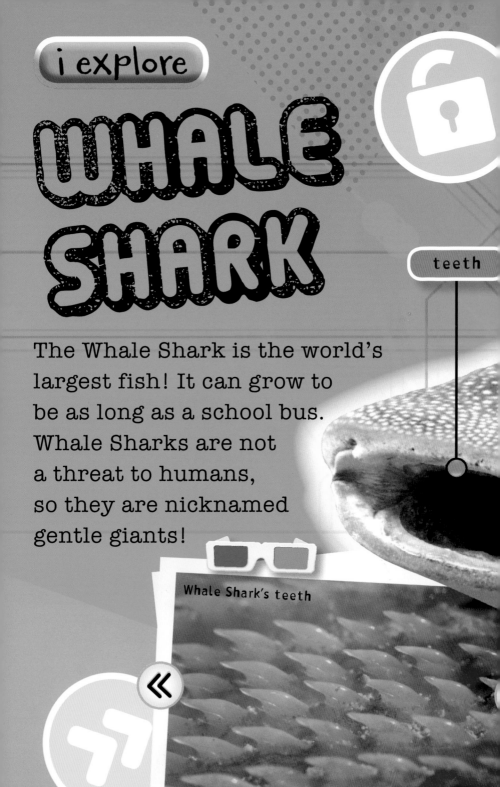

WHALE SHARK

teeth

The Whale Shark is the world's largest fish! It can grow to be as long as a school bus. Whale Sharks are not a threat to humans, so they are nicknamed gentle giants!

Whale Shark's teeth

ⓘ Whale Sharks have checkerboard patterns on their backs. These patterns are unique to each shark, just like fingerprints are unique to each human!

patterned skin

gill

→ **i learn** ✕

The Whale Shark is a filter-feeding shark. It has tiny teeth, so instead of biting its food, it sucks water into its mouth and then pushes it out through its gills, trapping any food in its gill plates.

i explore **MORE**

Basking Shark

Whale Shark with diver

i discover

All filter-feeding sharks
are slow swimmers.
Basking Sharks move at
around 2.5 mph (4 kph),
which is slower than a
human walking!

HAMMERHEAD SHARKS

The hammerhead shark takes its name from its hammer-shaped head. This unusual head cuts through the water, making it easier for the shark to change direction as it swims.

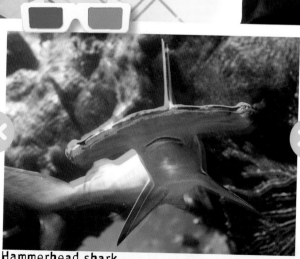

Hammerhead shark

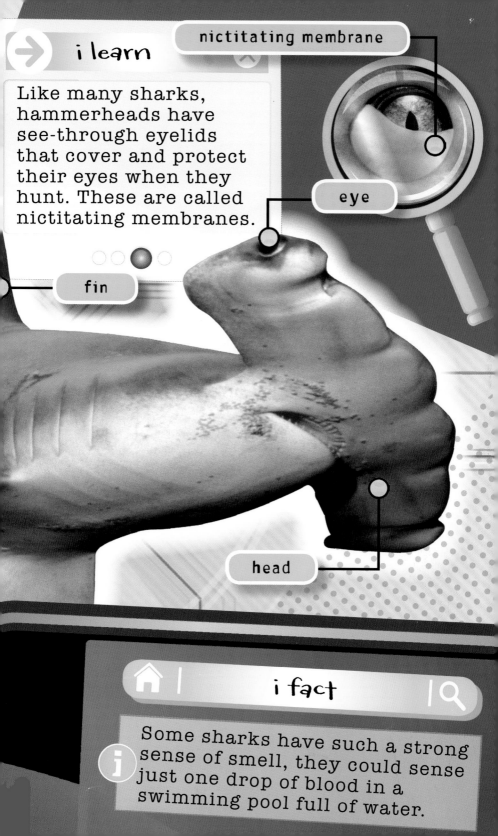

nictitating membrane

Like many sharks, hammerheads have see-through eyelids that cover and protect their eyes when they hunt. These are called nictitating membranes.

eye

fin

head

i fact

Some sharks have such a strong sense of smell, they could sense just one drop of blood in a swimming pool full of water.

SILVERTIP SHARK

Different sharks have their pups in different ways – some lay eggs, while others, like the Silvertip Shark, carry their pups inside them. Once a shark is born, it is left to fend for itself.

🏠 | i facts | 🔍

ℹ All species of sharks grow up knowing how to hunt without being taught.

An empty shark egg is called a mermaid's purse.

Mermaid's purse

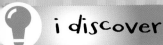
Mother bullhead sharks lay spiral-shaped eggs. They push the eggs between rocks to keep them safe.

Bullhead shark's egg

mother shark

pup

i learn

While a Silvertip Shark pup is inside its mother, it is connected to its mother by a cord. This cord gives the pup food and oxygen. When the pup is born, the cord breaks and the pup swims away.

BLACKTIP REEF SHARK

Just like humans, sharks need oxygen to survive. The Blacktip Reef Shark must keep water flowing over its gills to "breathe." To do this, it swims constantly.

mouth

⌂ | i fact | 🔍

ⓘ All sharks have between five and seven pairs of gills.

Like many sharks, the Sandtiger Shark can "breathe" when it is still. It does this by gulping water into its mouth and then pumping the water over its gills.

dorsal fin

Sandtiger Shark

gills

i learn

Sharks "breathe" by pushing water through their gills. Oxygen is taken in from the water and carried around the shark's body by its blood.

23

UNUSUAL SHARKS

Some sharks do not look like sharks at all, but all sharks have a skeleton made of cartilage, many rows of teeth, five to seven pairs of gills, and skin covered in denticles.

whiskers

→ i learn

The Tasseled Wobbegong Shark has a beard made of whiskers that look like seaweed or coral. The beard camouflages the shark so it can attack and eat small fish that come close!

i discover

The Cookiecutter Shark takes its name from the cookie-shaped holes it leaves in its victims. It does this by sucking onto the prey with its lips, then cutting out circles of flesh.

Cookiecutter Shark

Tasseled Wobbegong Shark

Dwarf Lantern Shark

i facts

The Dwarf Lantern Shark only grows to 8 in (21 cm) long. That's about the size of an adult's hand!

Saw Shark

A Saw Shark has a long snout with teeth along the edges. It uses its snout to kill other fish.

🏠 | i fact | 🔍

Zebra Sharks rest on the seabed during the daytime and hunt during the night.

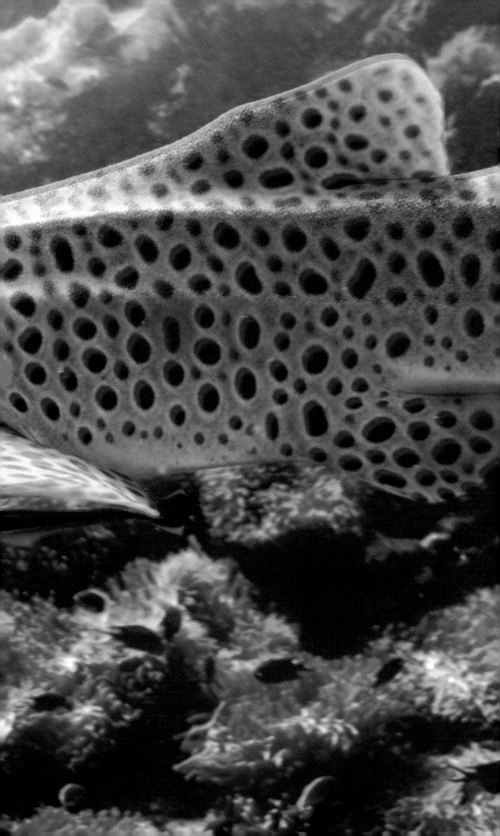

ENDANGERED SHARKS

Many sharks are in danger of becoming extinct. This means that the number of these sharks in the wild is falling and they might die out completely.

Great White Shark

i fact

The Great White Shark is famous for being the most terrifying shark of all, but its numbers are dropping due to human actions!

→ i learn ⊗

Sharks are hunted and killed by humans for their fins. After their fins are cut off, sharks are thrown back into the sea, where they die. The fins are then sold for shark fin soup or to make traditional medicines.

Hammerhead shark without fins

Shark fins

i discover

Megalodon lived 1.5 million years ago! This shark looked very similar to the Great White Shark, but it could grow up to 82 ft (25 m) long, which is longer than a truck! The Megalodon is thought to be the biggest shark that has ever existed.

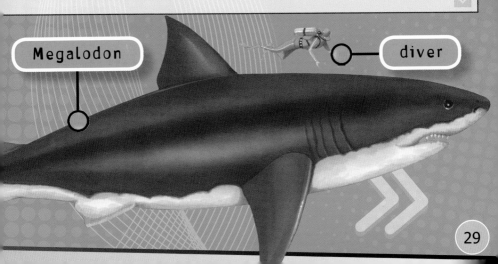

Megalodon

diver

i explore FACTS

Sharks have been on earth for over 400 million years, which means they were around before dinosaurs!

Sharks try their food before they eat it. If the food is too bony for them, they let it go. This might be why most people survive shark attacks!

The Shortfin Mako is the fastest shark in the ocean. It can travel at about 46 mph (74 kph).

Every year, more people die from bee stings than from shark attacks.

Most shark attacks on humans occur along the coasts of the United States.

Every year, humans kill up to 70 million sharks. On average, sharks kill fewer than 10 people each year.